Enslaved By Consumption

Dominico Johnston

Acknowledgements

To every family member and friend who taught me the value of a dollar.

Brian Johnson - Edits, ideas and review.

TheMarketCapitalist.com's Visitors - Your readership is appreciated and motivational.

Contents

Preface

One / To Stand on the Shoulders of Giants

Two / The Unquenchable Need

Three / What Matters Most?

Four / The Power of Debt

Five / Getting the Fiscal House in Order

Six / Release Thy Shackles!

Seven / Final Thoughts

Preface

Our philosophy of life, habits, perceptions, and desires shape how we live our lives. Our thoughts and actions shape who we are individually. Cumulatively, they shape our family life and our society as a whole. Since our modern industrial age, man has found himself on an unfamiliar playing field. A growing abundance has become accessible to a growing number of people. In the midst of this abundance, man has become lost in a world of consumption. He has become so drunk with consumer lust that he has willingly enslaved himself.

A prominent vein of thought that is readily present throughout our modern society is the notion that consumption is king. As a result, far too many of us have bought into believing that the crescendo of life's greatness is to be had by obtaining the maximum amount of consumer goods and services. Whether it is houses, cars, recreational toys, vacations, jewelry, clothes or some other good or service, we are now told that these items of desire should and can be ours.

Consumption is not without cost. Modern man has foregone the prudence of personal finance in his quest for more and more stuff. The wild world of debt financing has opened the doors to a million new possibilities for those with high to those with low income. Practically no adult is excluded from using debt financing to leverage their ability to consume. To many current day consumers, debt is the apple in the garden of personal finance. It is the promise that will enable life's dreams to come true, but for many debt is the snake that will leave its victim fiscally crippled and lame.

Whether we are young or old, with debt or without debt, each of us has the power to guide our financial futures toward the goals we seek to achieve. To sail toward and reach our financial goals, we must have discipline.

Today's personal finance topics are often composed of recipes. Financial advisors are paid to insist you save $X per year and invest in the market to provide you with a comfortable retirement by age 65. This advice is well and good, but only scratches the surface of the introspection that needs to be had amongst the majority of society. It is not that we lack the knowledge of what needs to be saved; the problem is we lack the will to save, the will to defer consumption, the will to say no to frivolous debt.

To cure our affliction we must understand the root causes of what is enabling detrimental patterns of behavior to shape and control our lives. To break the chains of enslavement, it is necessary for us to know how we arrived at this point in history, what is causing the problem to perpetuate itself and how we each can take action to reverse its progression. Breaking the chains of frivolous consumption must be done one-by-one, to not only create a better future for ourselves, but a better future for our entire society.

Chapter 1 – To Stand on the Shoulders of Giants

A historical sense is necessary for anyone to understand and appreciate their current state. If you have never experienced hunger, you do not have a true appreciation of a full stomach. Before we begin our journey, it is necessary for us to at least conceptually understand how the typical person lived only a few generations ago. In doing so, we will gain a partial perspective of how are current living conditions compare to our ancestors.

When we think of basic necessities for living, what comes to mind? Indoor plumbing (water and toilet facilities) and electricity. These necessities were luxuries less than a hundred years ago. For example, my grandfather, now 93 years old (born in 1922), was born in a sod house with a dirt floor in Iowa. The conditions sound as if I was describing some distant third world living situation or a primitive society from the Middle Ages.

If we were to somehow transport ourselves back to the turn of the 20th century, what would we likely find? How were families living in the early 1900's? In the U.S., one out of every 7 homes (14%) would have a bathtub, one in thirteen homes would have a telephone (8%), life expectancy was 47 years, only 144 miles of paved roads existed throughout the country, more than 95% of births took place at home, and two out of every ten adults could not read or write.

While the list of examples of what were normal living conditions in previous times is endless, it is important to maintain this point of reference. The very concept of poverty and being poor in our current society has been grossly distorted from our historical norm. To compare the two groups together is an exercise in absurdity.

Modern man's abundance of entertainment and technological distractions has led to an intellectual construct that is devoid of a historical sense of living standards. We have become like a young child that asks the age of an adult; a point of reference is absent that would provide meaning. Without a model of normalcy, no direction can be given as to what level consumption is excessive or is not excessive.

$$\$ \ \$ \ \$ \ \$ \ \$ \ \$ \ \$ \ \$ \ \$ \ \$ \ \$$$

When we hear the word poverty, we often think of people who lack food, warm housing, and have a meager amount of clothes. The average impoverished household in the U.S. today has a car with air conditioning, an average of two televisions, a cable/satellite subscription, an Xbox or PlayStation, refrigerator, oven and stove, microwave, clothes washer and dryer, ceiling fan, cell phone and a coffee maker. To boot, the average impoverished household in the U.S. has more living space than the average non-impoverished European household.

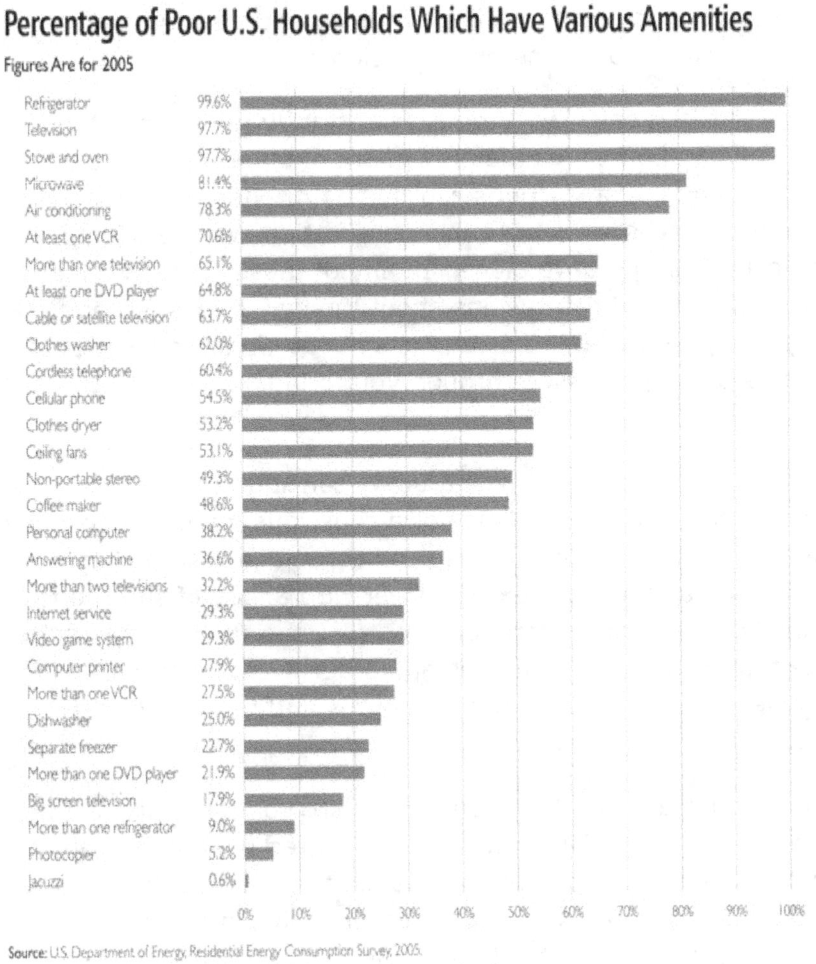

Percentage of Poor U.S. Households Which Have Various Amenities

Figures Are for 2005

Amenity	Percentage
Refrigerator	99.6%
Television	97.7%
Stove and oven	97.7%
Microwave	81.4%
Air conditioning	78.3%
At least one VCR	70.6%
More than one television	65.1%
At least one DVD player	64.8%
Cable or satellite television	63.7%
Clothes washer	62.0%
Cordless telephone	60.4%
Cellular phone	54.5%
Clothes dryer	53.2%
Ceiling fans	53.1%
Non-portable stereo	49.3%
Coffee maker	48.6%
Personal computer	38.2%
Answering machine	36.6%
More than two televisions	32.2%
Internet service	29.3%
Video game system	29.3%
Computer printer	27.9%
More than one VCR	27.5%
Dishwasher	25.0%
Separate freezer	22.7%
More than one DVD player	21.9%
Big screen television	17.9%
More than one refrigerator	9.0%
Photocopier	5.2%
Jacuzzi	0.6%

Source: U.S. Department of Energy, Residential Energy Consumption Survey, 2005.

The issue we face is the fact that within the history of man, nearly everyone in our current society is living in a state of abundance. Yet, whether well or not well off, we are almost always at a loss for this sense of abundance we should feel. We can comprehend where we stand historically, though in our day-to-day living we are lost to history and are trapped in the perception of the present day.

Why are we trapped in such a dilemma? Part of the problem can be attributed to what psychologists would call the recency effect. The effect is a cognitive bias that stems from receiving a disproportionate amount of recent observations toward one particular item, outcome or conclusion.

As we live our daily lives, we are constantly faced with the activities and other realities which are in place around us. These realities can be interactions with family, friends and co-workers, marketing messages, or simple observations we make while traveling from place to place. In any of these cases, we make observations and conclusions about the way things are and the way things should be. Expectations about life are a large part of what is being processed through your mind.

When we see the overwhelming majority of people driving by car from point A to point B, we naturally conclude that cars are the norm. For most of us, this is not a conscious mental conversation had within our thoughts. It is a subconscious assumption made. We do not affix our gaze on a street with a look of shock and think how radically different our current society is compared to one that was based on horses and other livestock transporting people. Instead we look at the vehicles and think, "Wow, I wish I had that car (or truck)!"

We live in the present and our minds are configured to deal with analyzing and handling much that is geared towards the short-term. It is not that we should change these preset inclinations and flip our mental processes in order to live in the past while in the present. The point is that we all must be aware that our mind's path of least resistance is to be consumed with day-to-day activity. Such a route may bring the greatest short-term satisfaction, but will lead to woeful long-term consequences and problems.

Let's take a step back and use another historical analogy to focus in on a point pertaining to our consumption dilemma. While the consumption we are discussing does not necessarily pertain to the consumption of food, a food analogy would be rather fitting to further emphasize our historical lesson.

With the advent of modern agriculture, society has experienced a transition where the majority of society existed in a rural setting to where the majority now exists in some form of an urban setting. A very small percentage of the population makes their living from agriculture and even fewer live in a rural area.

In times where most people survived based the land they owned and their ability to grow certain crops and raise livestock, the ability to consume food was limited. As people transitioned from the farm to the city, they were no longer dependent upon a set crops and livestock for sustenance. The grocery market became their source for their produce and livestock needs. This led to a greater selection of foods to choose from and eventually led to food becoming more affordable.

Changes in technology and large scale farming have led to supermarkets now having an abundance of food for their customers, along with an abundance of food choices one can select from. Few would argue that the increase in the availability of food and increase in its various forms has been a detrimental change.

The quest for food in each of us is driven by our appetite. When our body is in need of sustenance, we feel hungry and search out something to eat. By consuming a steak, candy bar, apple, carrot, pasta or other food we satisfy our body's need for energy in order for us to continue functioning normally and ultimately continuing to live.

As our society has developed and become wealthier across all classes of people, the most basic survival needs have become increasingly accessible. Today an abundance of food is available to all. For those deemed to be poor, food can be obtained for free via food bank offerings and electronic benefits transfer (EBT/Food Stamp) cards.

USDA expenditures for food and nutrition assistance, FY 1980-2013

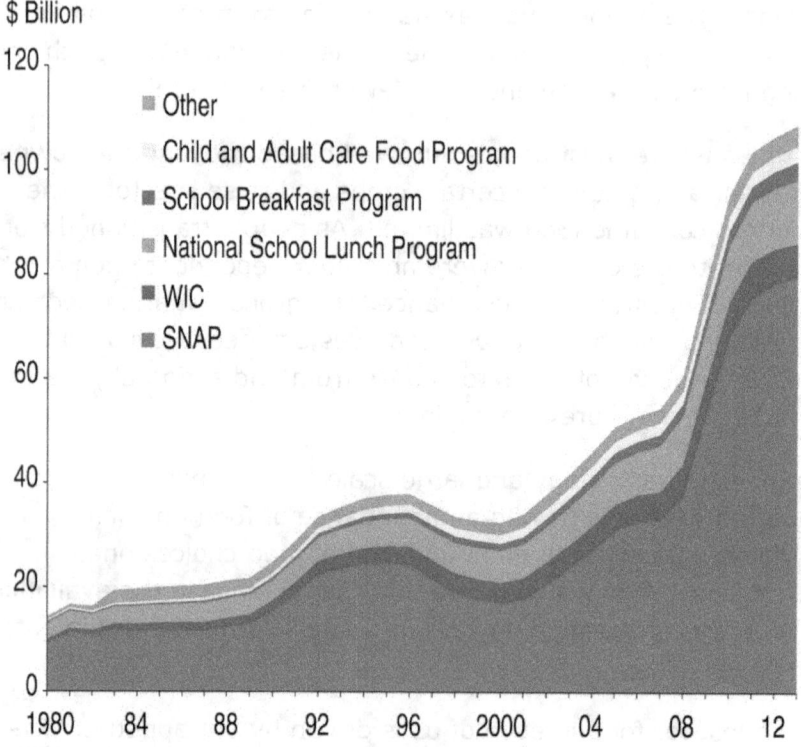

$ Billion

Legend:
- Other
- Child and Adult Care Food Program
- School Breakfast Program
- National School Lunch Program
- WIC
- SNAP

Source: USDA, Economic Research Service using data from USDA, Food and Nutrition Service.

Recent immigrants from third world countries serve as an example, too. These people arrive from impoverished countries to the abundance that is ever so prevalent throughout our society. The immigrants are skinny and often malnourished to a certain degree. Once they become acclimated to their new environment, it is not uncommon for obesity to set in. They swing from one extreme to another because they lack the governance to control their appetite. This is seen as a detrimental consequence of their new way of life.

The recent change (historically speaking) to a land with food in abundance has not changed our perception of what constitutes a healthy and fit person. Though we have food in abundance, we continue to view excessive eating as a social ill. Women's magazines do not showcase men with large stomachs and men's magazines do not showcase cellulite laden legs of women in order attract attention and increase sales. We naturally understand the connection between diet and body type and have a pretty consistent standard as to what an attractive and healthy body looks like.

The consistency as to what constitutes a reasonable standard of consumption is absolutely lost when we leave the realm of food and body type. The general message pushed either overtly or covertly is that more is better. Bigger, better and more luxurious is that which you should not only strive for, but that what which you deserve. Fit and lean is still admired in a person's body, but nowhere to be found in the realm of consumer spending habits.

Our consumer culture, just as our food culture, has come from a historic pattern of scarcity to one of abundance. In the process the consumer has not developed the governance needed to control the seemingly unquenchable appetite for more services and goods. The voice that speaks to control and moderation is weak and largely degraded by the chorus of marketers pushing greater consumption at every turn.

Relating the consumption of goods and services to our views about food consumption is a rather interesting comparison. In simple black and white terms, we understand food as one of the most basic necessities and most of the other things, outside water and shelter, as non-necessities. Yet, our behavior towards these non-necessities is often congruent with them being a necessity.

We are willing to forego our future purchasing power and bear the burden of debt's absurdly high interest rates to get today what we tell ourselves cannot wait until tomorrow. These actions compromise our future happiness and wellbeing. Our historical sense has been lost and our debt addiction has been turned to as the savior of our self-induced problems.

The weight of excess is the detrimental impact that comes from an unhinged consumer appetite. Frivolous debt must be serviced and detracts from other fiscally necessary activities such as saving for retirement, children's education, emergency reserves and other fiscal goals that take discipline to achieve. Progress is hampered just as the body's health is hampered from carrying and maintaining excess weight.

Whether it is how we live or how we eat today compared to our ancestors, the preponderance of society lives materially far beyond the dreams of society 100 years ago. As we continue our fiscal and philosophical exploration, it is imperative that we maintain our historical sense. Without it we are like a ship without a lighthouse.

Chapter 2 – The Unquenchable Need

Where is the line to be drawn?

If only we were able to readily distinguish our true needs from our wants, then maybe our consumption dilemma would not exist. Unless we experience some radical change in human nature, the hope of this enlightenment occurring is nothing short of a pipe dream.

The reality of our situation is that many of us, maybe even you, are overly convinced that we need an inflated amount of frivolous goods and services in order to feel content with life. This need could stem from status seeking, what some refer to as retail therapy, or a host of other self-satisfying stimuli. Whatever the cause is, each us of us must submit to the fact that we are adults, have free will and must face up to the consequences of the decisions we make.

Opportunity cost is an economic term that gets thrown around a lot in academic settings, yet is a concept that is woefully needed in the minds of anyone making a financial decision. Reality dictates that we all have a limited amount of resources. Resources can be time, money, energy or any other quantifiable item. When you choose to do a certain activity or buy a certain item, then something is given up. Whether we realize the foregone alternative or not, we have excluded something from occurring.

For example, if I were to buy a large television it may cost me $1,000. That $1,000 cannot be spent on a trip, some other good, service or saving that I had in mind. Whatever item was next in line is the opportunity cost of my television purchase. Though I have gained, I have lost, as well. What matters most is if my gain was truly worth the loss I incurred beyond the simple amount in dollars and sense.

Our personal finances represent the fountain unto which our thrust for consumption is quenched. The income we receive opens the door for these real and perceived needs to be met. In our modern times, society, through largely government intervention, has developed what is often referred to as a safety net. This net is designed to bring almost everyone up to a certain standard of living.

Food, housing, healthcare, childcare, direct income and the list goes on of other subsidies that are provided at varying rates to establish a certain baseline within society.

The focus here is not to debate the merits of such programs, but to make understood that this safety net exists and its ramifications to our consumption habits and personal finance choices.

As with a trapezes artist in a circus, a net enables the actor to engage in stunts that would most likely not be engaged in, if the safety of the net did not exist. Our social needs net has a similar impact on the actions of those in our society.

For those existing off the cushion of the net, qualities such as prudence and frugality are often lost. The guarantee of life's 'basics' brings a sense of comfort that retards the drive to excel in one's personal and professional life. This is a horrible outcome for those directly affected, but its detrimental effects spread beyond the direct recipients.

We cannot help but notice the activities that occur around us. Our senses trap us to seeing, smelling, hearing and feeling what is occurring. Our entire perception of the world as we know it is driven by what we perceive via our senses. When we witness activity that is incongruent with what we are taught and believe, then our worldview must be realigned with our new found reality.

When we see low income childcare centers with luxury automobiles picking up children, food stamp recipients buying choice cuts of meat and welfare recipients with smartphones, the observations have an impact on the psyche of the entire society.

Whether we like it or not, these observations have a profound impact on the way we view and know the world around us.

A leveling has occurred in society and the ripple effect can be mostly felt in the layers of middle class workers. While in college I worked at a Target store. For many of the employees, the first day of the month was one of the most distained and unsettling times. It was the time when these low income workers had to witness welfare recipients come through and buy things the workers struggled to afford. It was disillusioning for them. Most of the workers were not in college. As far as they could see, their career was limited to being a floor worker in a Target store.

To move beyond their limited incomes, most workers would engage in two behaviors. First, they would expend all the money they would take home. The concept of saving had become a stranger that was rarely invited into the mind's thought process. Secondly, they would leverage their money through purchases on credit. These purchases could range from cars to the shoes on their feet. Their solution for surpassing those below them was not through strategic long-term planning, but frivolous short-term spending.

The problem noted above stretches throughout incomes all the way into the top 5% of earners. The truth that was never told either on purpose or because the connection was never made is that the wage you earn from working and your consumption are the equivalent to a hound chasing a rabbit on a track. As long as the rabbit stays slightly ahead of the hound, all is well. A perpetual chase with no end in sight is a reality you are to live.

Placing the need to feverishly consume above the many other priorities that exist in one's life comes back to the pesky concept of opportunity cost. Whether you make $30,000 a year or $130,000, we all can find an endless list of different things to blow our money on. If discipline and forethought do not exist, then all the money in the world cannot save us.

$ $ $ $ $ $ $ $ $ $ $

What you might have noticed by this point is the problem we are facing is not so much a money problem. The problem of consumption is a *priority* problem. We can all talk about money and inequality until we are blue in the face. What we really need to talk about is the inequality of planning that is vacant in our minds.

The human race is supposedly the most advanced creature in the animal kingdom. Yet, by our behavior we often exude less forethought than exists within the mind of a squirrel. When winter is approaching squirrels take it upon themselves to find nuts and seeds and place them in crevices of trees or holes in the ground where they can be retrieved at a later date. Squirrels know how to plan and how to save.

Whether we can admit it to ourselves or not, we do not live in Disney's Magic Kingdom. Things in life can and will go wrong on an individual level and a larger societal one. We may go through many 'winters' in our life, just as a squirrel will. In those instances, it is the completed preparation that can make bad situations manageable. If preparation has been lacking, then bad situations can become absolute tragedies that scar us for the rest of our lives.

In 2009 the U.S. economy was in the throes of recession. At the time I had been working for County Bank, a community bank headquartered in central California. The bank had experienced significant growth in the previous twenty years and most recently had benefited from the housing boom, which was quite strong throughout the entire state of California. For a number of reasons, when the recession hit, the bank was very unprepared to weather the storm. In February of 2009 County Bank was taken over by the FDIC and its accounts were transferred to WestAmerica Bank.

I worked in an internal department and within weeks of the takeover, our entire department's staff was laid-off. This was not good news and certainly was not a joyous occasion at all. The difference between me and many of my counterparts that experienced a loss of employment during the Great Recession is the fact that I had taken and foregone taking certain actions. I had been prudent in my financial planning.

At the time I was laid off, I had over one year's savings sitting in a savings account that could we withdrawn at a moment's notice. Not only was my balance strong in my savings account, my expenses were controlled to the point that I did not have to worry about overly burdensome on-going costs. Debt had not become my master.

As a result of not feeling the weight of debt on my back, I was not forced to take a job simply for a paycheck. The recession produced great scarcity in the job market. Simply finding an opportunity was difficult. If income was needed, I would have almost certainly had to settle for much lower paying job that did not help me develop the skills I had gone to school to acquire. It also would have likely caused me to commute further or relocate.

With time I was able to find a job that paid slightly higher than the position I previously held at County Bank. Not only that, but it was in a field that enabled me to develop my financial and data related skills. In short, I was able to maintain my level of income and advance my career because I put myself in a position where my finances did not dictate my job search.

$ $ $ $ $ $ $ $ $ $ $

When we realize the unquenchable need is not unquenchable, then we begin to take control and bring our lives in order. The quest to stretch ourselves to our financial limits is no different than redlining a car's engine continuously. It might be thrilling and fun for a while, but it can only last so long before it becomes a stress for the engine, the chasse and the driver.

We do not exist in some amorphous state where thoughts are thrown at us and we are at their mercy to react. Remember, we are the most advanced being in the known universe. We may make crazy decisions and act irrational at times, but we have the ability to accomplish amazing feats. Overcoming the hypnotism of our consumer culture is one of the feats each of us has the power to achieve.

As we noted previously, when food came into abundance most of were able to control our eating habits to fend off obesity. This same situation is possible with our discretionary income. We do not have to be victims of consumption obesity. When discretionary income expanded to the point where we now can buy an unimaginable variety of goods and services, it did not mean we had to bow before each gizmo and pay homage via our hard earned money and debt funding. The power of decrement is ours and ours to use in defending against the unquenchable need to consume.

Self-control is not a bad word. Potty training may have been a burdensome experience when we were a toddler, but as adults we would be unable to function in society without such self-control. What is uncomfortable at first is not necessarily something to be labeled as bad and shunned. Growth often times takes effort and it is only once we have grown that we can see how limited we once were.

Chapter 3 – What Matters Most?

For some, priorities are like the Rock of Gibraltar; prominent and unyielding. For others, priorities are like Gumby; flexible and ever-changing. When it comes to setting financial goals, they need to be more like Gibraltar and less like Gumby. A sound personal finance plan is not built upon gambling or any other get rich quick scheme. You must have discipline and be steadfast in your convictions.

To begin with, every family and individual should ask themselves "What matters most?" What do you want to accomplish in life? What are your goals? I can almost guarantee the majority of the goals will have some critical financial component. Also, I can almost guarantee, if thought about through serious reflection, the goals will be heavily weighted towards the long-term.

What are typical examples of long-term goals people have?

- Homeownership / Buying a larger home
- Retiring by a certain age
- Starting and raising a family
- Saving for college
- Starting a business
- Buying a plot of land or a vacation home

As you might have noticed, all the goals above and other similar goals you can think of do not happen over the course of a few days, weeks, months or even sometimes years. They take substantial preparation and often need some form of regular maintenance once they are obtained. These are goals that are not represented by a specific point in time, such as a vacation, but span over a range that might be able to be loosely defined or not defined at all. These are goals that, more likely than not, will have a defining impact on your life and possibly the life of others.

To reach these life goals, we must tune out the waves of consumer temptation that come our way on a daily basis. A million products and services exist to meet some tangible or intangible need and all of them want us to want them. With a loose wallet those million products and services will quickly erode away at whatever money we have and steal the long-term dreams we have set.

The will to power must be exercised in the spirit that the late German philosopher Frederick Nietzche set out before us. Our will, our internal fortitude, must be harnessed in order to be our driving force in achieving the goals that matter most to us in life. We must reach the point where we are able to speak about such goals without having day-to-day distractions knock us off our focus as we progress towards the goals we have set before us.

Setting goals is not an annual New Year's resolution list that is forgotten about in a few weeks. It is a continual process that is evaluated and measured for reasonableness and progress.

As with any voyage in life we take, we need some type of road map if we are to achieve success. Establishing a process and breaking down items into manageable pieces will provide a structure in which our goals can be defined and a method in which they can be monitored.

A structure that can be followed in order to craft your own road map to success is as follows:

- List out what major goals you want to achieve in your life

- Define why you want to achieve each goal

- For each goal, create an approximate timetable

- List resources that will be needed to achieve your goals

    o Time
    o Money
    o People
    o Knowledge/Skills
    o Identify milestones and measurements of success

Going through the exercise listed above enables you to think beyond the day-to-day obligations we all face. It is a process that goes beyond the fiscal in order to describe a real pathway in which we want to venture down on the road called life. Knowing where we want go and what we want to do gives us a point of reference that goes beyond having trivial consumption patterns that we have become addicted to.

For too many people, even when presented with the goal frame work listed above, the time in which to begin progressing towards their goal is always just over the horizon. "When I make $X, then I'll start saving for retirement (or some other life event)." The bitter truth is that these changes in income level being pondered are much more dramatic in one's mind than what they are when they actually occur. Spending a little more here and a little more there incrementally creeps up and suddenly when that income level is reached reality sets in. The glut of free cash flow that was foreseen is not nearly as big as what was dreamed. Perception and reality can differ greatly.

I have, on a first hand basis, listened to people making in the top 5% and above of all earners in the U.S. lament about not being able to contribute near the IRS's maximum allowable amount to their retirement fund. Why is this? It is not that the income simply does not exist for these people. They are making individually well over $100,000 annually. It stems from choices made in the past and present that continually place consumption ahead of saving. They are forever chasing the horizon.

No one says they want to endlessly chase a dream. People talk about living their dreams. To taste the sweetness of success is what we envision. Allowing our uncontrolled whims to dictate our life does not bring us to the point where we can live our dreams. Recognizing that certain actions are of greater value than others is the turning point where we can truly identify what matters most in our lives and start living in accordance with those values.

Chapter 4 – The Power of Debt

Debt can create a Cinderella at the ball or the ragamuffin after the clock strikes twelve. The primary lesson to remember about debt is that it is neither good nor bad. Debt is a tool just as the hammer in your garage is a tool. You can put up a fence with a hammer or go knock out your neighbor's car window. Debt behaves in the same way. It is a vehicle for you to achieve something. Your decisions dictate whether that achievement is helpful or harmful to your life.

If you are a working individual, you most likely have already used debt in some form to obtain some type of product or service. Debt comes in many flavors and transcends the scope of personal finance into the business and corporate world. For our discussion we will focus on the personal side of the house.

Off the top of your head, what are some forms of debt you are familiar with?

Here is a brief list:

- **Mortgage**

   A mortgage is an instrument of debt, which is secured by the collateral of specified property. The borrower is obliged to pay back with a predetermined set of payments. Mortgages are used by individuals and businesses to make large real estate purchases without paying the entire value of the purchase up front. Over a period of many years (often 30), the borrower repays the loan, plus interest, until they eventually own the property outright. Mortgages are also known as "liens against property" or "claims on property." If the borrower stops paying the mortgage, the bank can foreclose.

- **Home Equity loan**

  A home equity loan (or second mortgage) is a consumer loan secured by a second mortgage. The loan allows a homeowner to borrow against the equity they have in their home. The loan is based on the difference between the homeowner's equity and the home's estimated market value. This form of loan sometimes allows for the interest payments to be tax deductible.

- **Home Equity Line of Credit**

  A home equity line of credit is basically a line of credit secured by your home. When the line of credit is drawn down, the financial institution providing it places a second mortgage loan on your home until the loan is paid off. If the loan is not paid off, your home could be sold to pay off the remaining debt. Interest rates on such loans are usually adjustable rather than fixed. The loan rates are almost always lower than what you would find offered by a credit card.

- **Auto Loan**

  Your run of the mill auto loan will be obtained from a local bank, credit union or the auto dealer selling the vehicle. More often than not, the credit union will be able to offer you the most competitive interest rate. The interest paid on an auto loan is not deductible from your federal income tax.

- **Payday loan**

  A type of short-term borrowing where an individual borrows a small amount at a very high rate of interest. The borrower typically writes a post-dated personal check in the amount they wish to borrow plus a fee in exchange for cash. The lender holds onto the check and cashes it on the agreed upon date, usually the borrower's next payday. These loans are also called cash advance loans or check advance loans. The rates and fees associated with payday loans make credit card lending look sane.

- **Credit Cards**

A card issued by a financial company giving the holder an option to borrow funds, usually at point of sale. Credit cards charge interest and are primarily used for short-term financing. Interest usually begins one month after a purchase is made and borrowing limits are preset according to the individual's credit rating. It is not out of the ordinary to see a debt service rate of 20% for carrying a balance on a credit card. A consumer is more likely to rack up debt using a credit card (as opposed to other loans) because credit cards are widely accepted as currency because it is psychologically easier to hand someone a credit card than to fork over the same amount in cash.

- **Personal Loans**

Personal loans are offered by most banks, and the proceeds may be used for virtually any expense (from buying a new phone to paying off a bill). Typically, personal loans can range anywhere from a few hundred to a few thousand dollars. As a general rule, lenders will require some form of income verification, and/or proof of other assets worth at least as much as the individual is borrowing. According to the Federal Reserve, interest rates on these loans average around 10 - 12% and are to be paid back within two years.

- **Cash Advances**

Cash advances are typically offered by credit card companies as short-term loans. Other entities, such as tax preparation organizations may offer advances against an expected IRS tax refund or an anticipated future income earned. Such loans are typically not tax deductible, only a few hundred dollars and come with high related interest rates and fees. Along with payday loans, they should be a lending mechanism of last resort.

From our brief tour of personal debt options, it is not difficult to find a way or need that debt cannot seem to satisfy. For decades, financial institutions have developed different methods of loaning money to customers in order to meet their needs. The costs differ and the terms differ, but in the end all these offerings constitute debt; a future financial obligation you make in order to meet an immediate need.

$ $ $ $ $ $ $ $ $ $ $

It is not hard to see the power of debt at work. If you own a home or car, you can probably see debt at work from where you sit. Most big ticket items, such as homes and cars are purchased through taking on some degree of debt. Without debt financing it would take considerably longer to buy a home or car.

Consider buying a home for $250,000. If your household income was $60,000 annually and you managed to save $25,000 per year after taxes, it would take you 10 years to save enough to buy the house (The example does not consider the possibility of interest investment income earned from saving the money in a bank or brokerage account.). In this instance debt solves the dilemma through providing 80% or sometimes more of the asking price via loaned funds. Therefore, the situation dramatically changes. Saving $50,000, or 20% of the cost, would only take two years.

When debt is used correctly, it can be a powerful and very helpful tool in making dreams into a reality. Joyful images of new homeowners are easy to imagine. Debt's other side is equally as true and can be horribly grotesque. Financial strain creates stress, which can lead to ruined dreams, unhappy lives, abuse, drug addiction, health problems, divorce and even suicide. The loss of one's fiscal control is really only the tip of the iceberg as to what negative impact debt can cause.

It is the responsibility of each of us when we take on debt that the debt we shoulder does not create nightmares rather than dreams. Reflecting back on the long-term goals that we have set forth, it cannot be stressed enough that the actions we take today and those we take tomorrow and so on will either lead us toward or away from what we want reality to be in 5, 10, 25, 40 or 60 years from now.

When debt is used frivolously, we can quickly be sucked into a vortex that seems impossible to escape. Just as quicksand slowly pulls its victim down into its unyielding trap, unchecked debt can pile up to unimaginable levels.

Debt that is not controlled and serviced regularly will cause a disaster. Let me say it again...Debt that you do not control and payoff according to the plan you originally had when you took on the debt is the start of a nightmare. Such a situation is a game changer in the truest since of the term. No longer are you using debt to obtain some good or service, debt is now using you. Debt becomes the master and you must compromise your wishes and desires to meet the master's need.

In modern societies the traditional form of slavery in which one person owns another person has been expunged. A new form of slavery is present and growing. It is a voluntary form of slavery that comes through fiscal channels. The inability to control ones consumption habits and the allure of debt to satisfy short-term needs continues to cause an epidemic of voluntary enslavement.

Being owned by a master called debt is no way to live life. Enslavement by consumption is a pitiful state. To willingly throw away your future for it is a remarkably sad idea to entertain. This idea though is a reality for many of our family, friends and co-workers. It is not a state we say is reserved for those on the fringes of society. No, it is a state that afflicts many 'regular' people.

If the words I'm using seem harsh or maybe exaggerated, then a simple example will help to convey the reality behind my preachy tone.

Credit cards are a very mainstream form of debt that it used by millions of people. If the user abuses the credit they are given via the card, they can find themselves and their family in a world of hurt. What might seem like a nominal purchase can have very large repercussions over the long haul.

For this example, let's assume you have gone out and bought an 80 inch television for $2,500. The cost was charged to your credit card and you have decided you will pay for the expense in increments of $50 per month. This might seem affordable, but it is actually terribly irresponsible and expensive.

If we assume that the annual percentage rate (APR) for the card is 18%, a pretty reasonable assumption, we can determine what the true long-term cost of the purchase will be. First, it is important to realize that the $50 payment is not going to go entirely to the principle cost of the purchase. The 18% ARP is a cost that must be accounted for every month, in addition to the repayment of the purchase amount.

Doing the math on the debt reveals that the $50 monthly payment would breakdown into $38 going towards fulfilling the cost of interest and $13 toward the $2,500 liability. Carrying this payment schedule on to the end of its life would create a situation where it would take 28 years to expunge the debt. The amount of interest paid would be $5,897, which would make the television actually cost $8,397. This amounts to over 3.3 times the original cost of the television.

The above situation is staggering in its own right, but it is not the entire picture. By paying a credit card company debt payments over and over again, you are foregoing what could have been achieved with the debt service money being expended. Remember the concept of opportunity cost? This is a voluntary form of enslavement that may not even be realized by the person who is enslaved.

If you would have invested $50 a month for 28 years and earned 7% annually on your investment, you would have nearly $50,000 in the end. Opportunity costs are real whether we realize them or not.

A person high on debt is comparable to a weary traveler in the desert. A distant mirage may bring hope of an oasis, while the reality is only a long, tiring and hot path ahead. The repayment of debt is the long path and the interest that must be borne is heat and exhaustion from having to travel along the path. Such an experience will inevitably scar us emotionally and change the course of one's life; whether it is realized or not.

Chapter 5 – Getting the Fiscal House in Order

One substantial obstacle for individuals and families in gauging their economic health is the lack of a golden rule to guide us in determining fiscal health. We all have different incomes, obligations and aspirations. These various factors influence our abilities and needs in the present and future. Even though a golden rule might not exist, we can develop constructs to help us assess our situation to ensure it is in line with our desired outcomes.

In 2014 it was estimated that 35% of American's had a debt that was delinquent. That means that around 77 million Americans have a debt that has not been serviced in over 180 days. The amount of debt, on average, was $5,200 and includes credit card bills, child support, medical bills, utility bills, parking tickets and membership fees. It is extremely likely that you or someone you know have a fiscal obligation that needs to be addressed.

Even without a golden rule, we all understand that delinquent debt is a fiscal issue that needs to be addressed. Financial matters, as with most other instances in life, are easy to diagnose when things have already gone bad. Yet, for yourself and the rest of society, pointing to a problem once it has occurred is not good enough. Just as students are taught defensive driving, we want to be wise enough in our financial activities to avoid calamity.

Why does such a large swath of the population have a delinquent debt? We all understand that to live we must consume. Yet, we all have the ability at some level to choose what we will and what we will not consume. We are free to choose and from the looks of the data presented above, a sizable portion of society finds it difficult to control their level of consumption. To get our house in fiscal order, the first place we must check on is the noodle between our ears.

To understand the problem we face, we must look deep inside the recesses of our collective psyche. The Western mind, and more specifically the American mind, is generally predisposed to a particular worldview when it comes to the part of life commonly referred to as "Keeping up with the Jones'." The measure of one's success is tethered to specific tangible items that large portions of society race towards like a dog chasing a cat. The house, the car, the clothes, the toys, the jewelry, the vacations and the list goes on and on.

What does success look like to you? Is it a list of tangible items, such as those noted above? If so, you are not out of the ordinary and it is not necessarily a bad thing. Consumption is not an evil unto itself. We must remember that the problem we want to eradicate is the detrimental methods often employed to foster our consumption habits. Man's natural desire for progress should not be retarded, but man's natural inclination for reckless abandon should.

At some point in human development, the idea of self-deprivation came to be known. Putting off an activity until tomorrow in order to prepare for it today was recognized as virtue, not as a foolish strategy. Planning and forethought have brought about many amazing human accomplishments; from construction of Egypt's Great Pyramids in ancient times to space exploration in modern times.

We have developed an acute sense to envision the world of tomorrow and then begin to craft the vision with the actions we take today. Yet many of today's cultural currents seek to erode this human faculty and transform us back into a more primitive creature set on living hand to mouth. In the process these currents seek to strip man of his freedom and place him back into a form of voluntary enslavement. Placing us in a state where were "keeping up with the Kardashian's" or some other media icon who we neither know nor share hardly anything in common with.

To keep up with such icons and have those things we have convinced ourselves we so badly need takes resources. When we are faced with the reality of our limited resources and our endless wants, we find ourselves faced with a choice. The choice hinges upon either delaying consumption until more resources are in hand or venturing down a more risky path. Utilizing the power of debt brings risk and can easily become a reckless tool, unless properly managed and controlled.

Where did we come from and how did we get to this point are two pivotal perspectives to have when dealing with the current epidemic of frivolous consumption fueled by debt. The topic of personal finances is all too often confined to budgetary issues, while wholly disregarding the psychological and philosophical underpinnings driving actions and decisions. Whether you personally are dealing with debt and spending habits that have become unmanageable or are concerned with the path our society is lumbering down, it is crucial to understand that the concept of enslavement by consumption is only on the service an economic or personal finance issue. The root cause finds its foundation in psychological and philosophical precepts that have taken root in the collective unconscious of today's society. To eradicate this evil is to ensure our tomorrow is brighter than that of today.

$ $ $ $ $ $ $ $ $ $

How do we get our train of thought in proper order to avoid over consumption? First, we must have some point of reference to know what it would or would not be to over consume. Looking at the paycheck in your hands and concluding that staying within that maximum of consumption would leave out a large portion of our desires and aspirations.

The most universally applicable example of forethought needed when determining if we are or are not over consuming is the concept of retirement. Whether you are 21 or 61 we all know that one day we will either not care to work or will not be physically or mentally able to work. Therefore, our wage income must be assisted or replaced by some form of passive income.

To ensure a stream of passive income exists when we envision retiring, most set aside a certain amount of their wage income to be invested. The idea is that the income set aside plus the appreciation of the investment will result in a large enough amount of money that at the desired retirement date, the retiree can live off the stockpile and/or its regular returns.

To accomplish this feat we will employ a five step process of fiscal realization.

1. Where Am I?

2. Where Do I Want To Be and When?

3. How Do I Get To Where I Want To Be?

4. What Needs To Change?

5. How Do I Measure My Progress?

Example:

In our example we have an employed individual that is 40 years old. They have a spouse and two children. The children are eight and ten years old. The couple wants to retire at age 65.

Monthly take home pay is $5,000 for the wage earner and the employer pays for the family's health insurance plan, which is around a $900 benefit to the family. Mortgage, car and other regular payments cost approximately $2,000 per month and other expenses run an additional $2,000.

Each month the family can commit to saving $1,000 toward the goal of retirement. They are fearful that the promise of Social Security support will be gone or significantly compromised by the time they are able to benefit. Therefore, they are not factoring the potential funding from Social Security into their retirement equation.

To retire, the family estimates that they will spend roughly at the same level they do now, with a 2% annual inflation factor. They also assume their invested money will earn an average of 5% annually over 25 years.

With the information above we have a general understanding of where the family is financially and where and when they want to be there. The monthly savings allocation is the proposed mechanism to get them to the goal.

To answer the question of what needs to change, if anything, we must do a little analysis based on the information provided. In the chart below you will see a summary of the family's current state and where they end up given the monthly savings and inflation adjusted expenses.

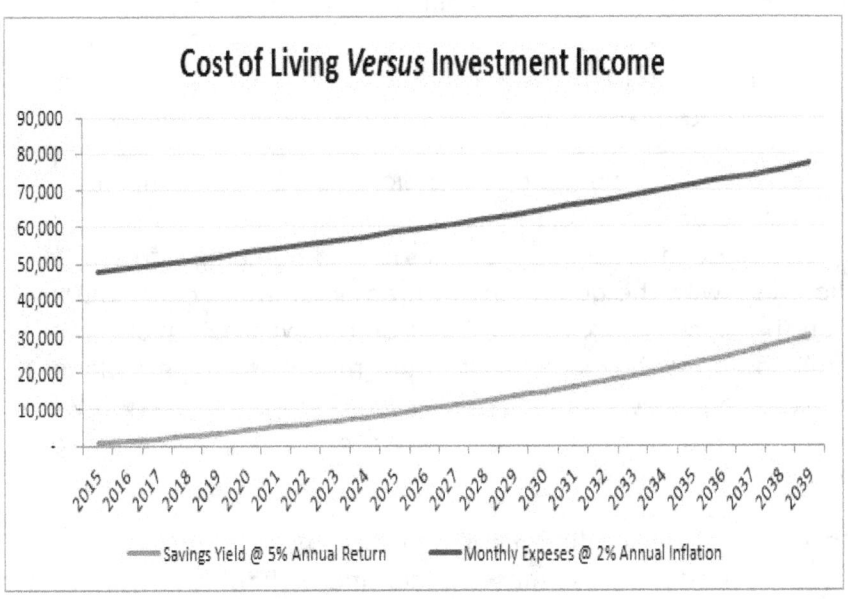

Our analysis shows that the savings and investment return plan does not pan out. Even if the couple kept their annual expenses at the same level today 25 years into the future, their investment's annual return would fall short of the current $48,000 of annual expenses.

When faced with the question as to what needs to change, it is important to not only focus on the first factor that comes to mind. For example, savings is the factor in focus here. Yet, savings is only part of the equation.

Why does the assumption about spending at a constant level year after year exist? After 25 years the home mortgage is probably paid off, which would erase a major monthly expenditure. What about expenditures associated with their two children? In 25 years, both children will be in their 30's and should not be dependent on their parents.

Unless some other purchasing priorities exist that will cause expenses to maintain or increase beyond current levels, multi-year commitments should decline by the time the couple is in their 60's. By the time retirement arrives, major spending moments in one's life should be years in the past. This is not something which happens automatically, but with a little planning and self-control should be a pattern that is easy to follow.

The reality of the example above dictates that some mix in savings, return on investment, or estimated future obligations must change in order to bring the desired outcome into alignment with the general plan. If an adjustment is not made then the plan is a joke and will not be followed by anyone in the family because they know it does not meet their expectations. It would be equivalent of us believing an Olympic athlete will win a gold medal when the athlete believes they lack the skill set to achieve a bronze medal.

Once a reasonable adjustment is decided upon, then a strategy for measuring progress must be identified. Thankfully, with this plan and any other financial plan you devise, the measure of success is quantifiable. Dealing with money has the benefit of being very exact and measurable.

In the couple's situation, they know their savings pathway and they know their spending pathway. As long as those keep inching in the right direction, they will achieve their goal. This might be a monthly, quarterly or bi-annual check-up.

Before we leave our example of the five step process, it is important to note that the measurement process is a tool to help you achieve your goal. It is not a tool to make you overly neurotic and crazed. If we reflect back on our example, it would be very unwise of the couple to look at the money they have invested on a daily basis. Most likely the investment bundle would consist of stocks and possibly bonds. Day by day changes could cause extreme mood swings and irrational decisions to be made. All the above would doom the ability of the couple to meet their long-term goal. Planning for the long-term more often than not means regular measurement on a paced basis.

$ $ $ $ $ $ $ $ $ $ $

With a framework to engage and direct your thoughts, the need for a golden rule becomes a trivial pursuit not worth pondering. As the decision maker in your life, you are able to take ownership of where you are today and where you want to be tomorrow. The sense and purpose you have defined will assist in helping to keep your mind straight as you deal with the multitude of daily distractions and temptations to throw you off your chosen path.

You will find yourself changing your thought process from asking, "Is that a good price?" to "Is that a good financial decision?" Lots of items and services can be quoted at competitive prices, but if our goals are larger than the accumulation of stuff, the luster of "a good deal" fades away fast. What can be a good deal for a particular item is ultimately a bad deal, if it takes you off the path to achieving your goal.

Setting financial goals is an affirmation that there is more to life than frivolous consumption whether or not it is fueled by debt. Debt can turn into our hemlock and frivolous spending alone can turn the straight and narrow path we once saw into a thousand winding roads. Whether debt or frivolous spending, either can cause our eyes fixation on what matters most to alter. The altering eye moves from the goals set and to some other distraction, which translates into failure for our stated aspirations.

If you are able to take command and get your house into fiscal order, you are among the elite. It may sound odd, yet it is unequivocally true. In a society that is fueled by endless consumption and short-sighted desires, being able to define your path in life and consistently work toward the pinnacles that you have set as a priority is a rare feat.

Chapter 6 – Release Thy Shackles!

The faculties endowed to each one of us provide the tools needed to live a life free of slavery and servitude. Even as we live in our Western societies that are free from the historic institution of slavery, from every direction we can hear the chains of voluntary enslavement rattling. It is a somber reality that harms not only those enslaved, but society as a whole.

Debt has its time and its place in helping people achieve accomplishments that may have taken decades to save for or may have been unattainable. Debt is a tool to be used by people, not a tool to use people. This truth has been lost amongst society. Our free will and unhinged desires have made us into kids at an unattended candy shop. In our eyes the world can and will be ours regardless of consequences, which we are too busy to be distracted by.

The idiocy of our perpetual adolescence must be broken. The fact that this trend of voluntary enslavement has been able to root itself so deep within our society speaks to the fact that we have successive generations failing to become fully self-sustaining adults. The most bewildering fact is that this reality has been borne not out of scarcity, but out of excess.

What does it mean to be a grown man or woman when you look in the mirror? Does it mean that you spend over a $200 a month on a cable TV, Internet and cell phone service, yet grift off the public dole using food stamps to sustain unhealthy eating habits? To rack up credit card charges and then turn to your parents for life's necessities when your monthly spending went a little too wild?

Is it that you go into foreclosure on a home that you no longer want because the home's value depreciated? Or knowingly rack up debt taking lavish vacations with the intent on declaring bankruptcy when the cards are maxed out? The list can go on and on.

Every one of these examples demonstrate people making fiscal choices that have voluntarily enslaved themselves to something or someone.   Whether it is the public, family, bank or creditor's debt, they have compromised their life because they could not control their fiscal desires and live up to the detrimental decisions they made.

Voluntary enslavement is not a characteristic of a brave culture, but a culture filled with cowards. In our case, we find that the fiscal aspect of our quandary means a culture filled with spoiled cowards. The problems faced, as seen in our examples above, are not contained to only those actors making the bad decisions. The contagion permeates throughout all institutions of society, just as an ivy vine steadily climbs up a tree depriving the tree of the ability to grow and flourish.

$ $ $ $ $ $ $ $ $ $ $

Whether it is you, a family member or a friend, we cannot sit idle and allow selfish and ill-advised financial choices drag down our society. No one walks down the streets and shouts "Enslave me! Enslave me!" The captors of consumption have altered the perception of so many within our society that shouting "Enslave me!" is not necessary. The seeds of unabashed material want and need have been planted and cultivated in the minds of all that through every voluntary action the unchecked desire pushes closer and closer to securing each shackle.

To release the shackles and find true financial freedom in our lives, we must look ourselves in the mirror and realize that we have the power to take full responsibility for our actions. We are our own fiscal masters.

Standing fiscally straight on our own two feet means breathing the sweet air of monetary freedom. For some the concept might be foreign or unrecognizable. If the thought does not resound within your soul, let me help breathe life into what this state of living looks and feels like.

Chasing a rainbow can bring momentary joy, but it ultimately is a pursuit of a vision that can never be grasped. This analogy is akin to what we do when we spend beyond our means to build a reality we have envisioned in our minds. Our consumption is our attempt to build something we cannot actually obtain. The use of debt provides the illusion that what cannot be had can be ours. For a momentary period the dream appears to be real.

As time marches on the promise of the rainbow transforms into an ominous thunderstorm. Debt's promise of making the unreachable reachable, soon turns into sand trap that slowly constricts our available options. The increased options to consume that once existed slowly transform into a greater and greater load on the back of the debtor. Servicing debt becomes the master and it must be served.

We do not need to chase rainbows. Beauty and happiness in life can be found all around us. Spending beyond our means to achieve some form of status or to achieve what we see as happiness in our lives is a delusion. To pull a carriage you put the horse before the carriage not the carriage before the horse. Certain things in life work well when done in a certain order. The principle is true with our spending habits. When we put our desire to consume before our ability to earn, we are setting ourselves up for failure.

Starting from the point of what we earn and then proceeding to consume puts our fiscal world on an axis that can operate smoothly and consistently. Operations are set in a natural manner, which by itself enables us to avoid many pitfalls. Finite earnings prescribe a border that tells us that our consumption habits are limited.

When we bring our lives into harmony with our spending habits, our view of the world changes. Controlled spending does not only mean not having to run to meet the demands of our debt master. Financial stability offers more than the release from a burdensome obligation.

Controlling ourselves empowers us to appreciate the things we do have rather than maintaining an endless fixation on what we do not have. Soon we find a greater appreciation of the things we do have that are of value. This path often goes beyond that which is consumable. What is often lost in a world where you must rush to meet a circus of fiscal obligations is that there is intrinsic value and joy to be gained from things you cannot necessarily place in your shopping basket.

Releasing yourself from the shackles of debt and mindless consumption means that you are able to see the material abundance that exists throughout our society. Every day we stand on the shoulders of giants that made such luxuries possible; electricity, television, the Internet, the internal combustion engine, and supply chain management in your grocery and department stores. These mechanisms of progress were meant to make life easier, not more frantic and burdensome.

In our state of abundance there is no reason to keep up with the Jones's or Kardashian's, just as there is no reason to gorge ourselves until we are sick from overeating. We do not live in a land of scarcity, but a land of plenty. The grim reaper of frivolous debt is not a pragmatic friend of ours and we have no business giving him control over our future decisions. The power comes from within each of us to either forego such a path or realize the error in our ways and stop following a path that leads to enslavement by our own consumption.

Chapter 7 – Final Thoughts

The way things are, are not the way things have to be. The lights of the city shine as do the lights in your home because of foresight and planning. Observing our surroundings will reveal to us a great many things that often times we assume exist as a given.

The state of our personal finances is no different than other aspects of our life. Where we fiscally stand today is not a product of chance. Each step we have taken in our past brought us to where we stand today. This revelation might be troubling to some, though it should not be. We are not but a feather in the wind. We have the ability to set our course and direct our life. Whether we are thrilled, content or unhappy with our personal finances, the good news is each of us has the power to change any dissatisfaction we may have.

Dealing with debt is like drinking; the right amount, at the right time and in the right place, you can find enjoyment. When that formula is off kilter, trouble can quickly take the place of enjoyment. All sorts of bodily and social ills can arise. A drinking problem is embarrassing, just as an indebtedness problem is embarrassing. No one wants to show their weaknesses.

Fixating on the fact that we have a problem is not where the success story is at. Realizing that each of us have the power to control and direct our personal finances is where the focus must rest. An opportunity for change exists for anyone that has found themselves in debt or lacks a debt problem, but cannot regulate their consumption habits. The opportunity is called freedom and it can be had by anyone.

In wanting all of these "things" what we are creating is a situation in which we willfully acquire more and more obligations. When the want of things comes prior to the assessment of an obligations value, we renege control our whims. The priorities we have set in our life must take a backseat because our desire to consume becomes the de facto priority.

The problem that we face within ourselves and throughout our society is a problem of priorities. The pressure and the call to align our actions to what our long-term goals are is lacking. Just as a doctor addressing a symptom may not be helping to cure the cause of a disease, personal finance issues that are confined to the realm of dollars and sense often overlook a deeper need that must be addressed.

The overarching worldview that governs mainstream through in our society must be altered from the course it has been on for decades. This goal is achieved through each one of us individually. The problem is not bigger than ourselves because the problem lies within each of us. The desire to consume beyond our hearts content must be looked at as a social ill, just as obesity is looked at as a social ill. Those with an issue should not be maligned or alienated, but they should not be looked at as normal or some weird part of what is included in our concept of "the American Dream."

Earning comes before having; not the other way around. The desire to earn more through hard work, education, or other legal means is a social benefit. When we are more productive we benefit, as well as society. Our earnings quantify this benefit and our spending or investing of the earnings is the byproduct. Inflating our purchasing power through frivolous debt is a cheat to ourselves and society. It is a burden taken that must be borne further down the road.

If you want to improve your life, build a better family, and help heal the world you live in, then take control of your personal finances. Expunging your addiction to debt and frivolous consumption will put yourself on a path to freedom, set a positive example for your friends and family, and help lighten the drag of misallocated resources throughout society. Change, whether big or small, starts within each one of us.

www.ingramcontent.com/pod-product-compliance
Lightning Source LLC
Chambersburg PA
CBHW072258200526
45168CB00016B/2126